SENTENCES OF JESUS
COMMENTED

Father John S. Mill

SENTENCES OF JESUS COMMENTED

50 phrases of Jesus Christ to reflect on

EDITORIAL
LETRA MINÚSCULA

May 2023
ISBN: 978-84-19867-23-0
Copyright © 2023 Father John S. Mill
Edited by Editorial Letra Minúscula
www.letraminuscula.com
contacto@letraminuscula.com

CONTENTS

PREFACE

The book you are about to read is a perfect gift for any Christian, offering a simple yet profound approach to the divine message. You can read this book alone or with your family, in the privacy of your home or with a small group.

If you want to become a better person, parent, spouse, child, or friend, you will find the moral foundations in this book to help you achieve it. Read each page calmly and, above all, ponder what you have read. Ask yourself how you can apply Jesus' words to your life and how you can grow as a human being with the help of love and true faith.

Jesus' message is everlasting because it deals with essential themes of human life: love, death, friendship, family, and more. I have selected some of his best-known thoughts to cover many subjects that may interest those who wish to understand the Christian message.

There are many false prophets and gurus eager to help us become better people, but there is only one true Master: Jesus of Nazareth.

In the words and actions of the Son of God, we find the deepest and most authentic wisdom—an eternal message that continues to inspire people all over the world throughout the centuries.

The immortality of the Christian message is based on the most important values any person can have love and faith. God loves us so much that He sent His Son to teach us the value of sacrifice, and the final victory of life over death, thanks to Jesus' resurrection.

This book is written with faith and humility. I have selected some of the most important words of Jesus for all those who wish to experience the Christian message anew. The comments I have added to each part of the divine word are a humble invitation for reflection. The wisdom we find in Jesus' ideas is so profound that we could write countless volumes about each of his statements, attempting to grasp their full depth.

Do not read this book as if it were a novel. It is not about reading, but rather reflecting on its contents. I recommend focusing on one thought a day. Choose a special time for yourself when you are calm, whether early in the morning or in the solitude of the night. Silence will help you connect better with your inner self and your soul. Read each sentence slowly and think about it. Ask yourself how you can apply it to your own life, how to become a better person, and how you can help others.

Many readers have been inspired by this book. I want to express my gratitude for your demonstrations of support and kindness. This book has helped the message of Christ become present again in many lives.

Father John S. Mill

1. FRATERNITY

"Whoever does God's will, who is in Heaven, is my brother, sister, and mother."

Matthew 12:50

We find a very powerful idea in this quote: fraternity. Those who do good works, those who behave ethically, those who follow God, and the teachings of His Son, Jesus, are not strangers; although we do not know them, they are our brothers and sisters. Additionally, those who go down the wrong path deserve our compassion. We should help them find Jesus in their lives and let them know that we are all children of God.

2. HELPING OTHERS

"The Son of Man came not to be served, but to serve and give his life as a ransom for many."
Matthew 20:28

Jesus did not come to our world to be adored or to live like a king in a palace full of servants. He came to be the humblest servant, to give His own life for us, and live as the simplest of men. If you want others to love you and to find a loving path in your life, you should help them. Forget about your selfishness and think about how you can help others. A life of service is one of the best ways to get closer to God.

3. THE WAY, THE TRUTH, AND THE LIFE

Jesus said to him, "I am the way, and the truth, and the life; no one comes to the Father, but through me."

John 14:6

The Son of God is three things. First, He is *the way*. There are many who claim to have the answers, false prophets and malevolent leaders who wish to pass for good. But there is only one leader, one true master: Jesus. Second, He is *the truth*. There is only one truth, which is that of God and His Son. Third, He is *the life*. God gave us life, and our lives should be devoted to following the word of God. To reach Him, there is only one way, one truth: Jesus.

4. BEING LIKE A CHILD

"Let the children come to me, and do not hinder them, because the kingdom of heaven is for those who are like them."

Matthew 19:14

What does it mean to be like a child? It means having enthusiasm for things, innocence, and not wanting to harm others. Children represent the best of humanity. They are eager to learn and have an innate curiosity about the world. They marvel at things, are creative, empathetic, and care about other people's feelings. They live in the present and are not obsessed with wealth or fame. For this reason, Jesus says that the kingdom of heaven belongs to children. Even as an adult, never lose the wonder or excitement of a child.

5. LOVE IS SACRIFICE

"For God so loved the world, that he gave his only begotten Son, so that everyone who believes in him should not perish but have everlasting life. God did not send his Son into the world to condemn the world, but that the world might be saved through him."

John 3:16-17

Love is about helping others. God sent Jesus into our world not to condemn us or make us obey, but to show us the path of love and sacrifice. Often, we must sacrifice ourselves for those we love. We do things we do not want to do for our loved ones to make them happy. Jesus gave His life as a gesture of love for humanity. God gave us His Son to teach us the true path to happiness. To love is to sacrifice for those we love; it is to give without expecting anything in return.

6. LOVE YOUR ENEMIES

"Love your enemies! Pray for those who persecute you! In that way, you will act as true children of your Father in Heaven. For He gives His sunlight to both the evil and the good, and He sends rain on the just and the unjust alike."

Matthew 5:43-47

Hate only breeds more hate, while love generates love. If you respond to hate with love, you can defeat evil. Many who once hated stopped doing so when they encountered love in return for hate, and kind words in response to harsh words. Do not let yourself be caught in the spiral of hate. Jesus' message is for every human being, both the good and the bad. Those who love God must put aside hate and help achieve the victory of Jesus on Earth through love.

7. SEEK AND YOU WILL FIND

"I tell you: ask and you will be given; seek and you will find; knock and it will be opened for you. For everyone who asks, receives; everyone who seeks, finds; and everyone who knocks will have the door opened."

Luke 11:9-10

Never give up. If you are looking for Jesus, you will find Him. If you want to overcome sadness, hopelessness, and hatred, God's love will help you find the way. Never grow weary of doing good works or pursuing the truth. It may be that in difficult moments you wish to stop seeking Jesus and abandon the path of faith. Do not give up; never stop knocking on God's door. God's house is always open to those who follow the teachings of His Son.

8. TO LEAD, YOU MUST SERVE

"Whoever wishes to become great among you must be your servant, and whoever wishes to be first among you must be slave of all. For even the Son of Man did not come to be served, but to serve, and give his life as a ransom for many."

Mark 10:42-45

Leadership is achieved by adding value to others. When we help make the world a better place and improve people's lives, others will follow us – not for our sake, but for their own. Leading is about serving and helping, not commanding, and being obeyed. Follow the way of Jesus: a path of sacrifice and service towards those in need.

9. DO GOOD WORKS

"Let your light so shine before men, that they may see your good works, and glorify your Father who is in heaven."

Matthew 5:16

Actions are more important than words. It is meaningless to say "I am good" when our actions contradict what we say. Each tree is known by the fruit it bears. People are better known for what they do rather than for what they say. Let your merciful light shine bright: do good works. When that happens, God will shine with you and be by your side. Following Jesus and helping those who suffer is the best way to praise our heavenly Father.

10. THE GOOD SHEPHERD

"The thief's purpose is to steal and kill and destroy. My purpose is to give them a rich and satisfying life. I am the good shepherd: the good shepherd who lays down his own life for his sheep."

John 10:10-11

Jesus brought us three things that we should never forget: life, abundance, and the example of his sacrifice. God gave us life, and Jesus teaches us His word. In His Son's teachings, everything is abundant because those who follow Him have the most important thing: love for others, for God, and for themselves. Jesus guides us in the good life. The thieves, the evildoers who do not follow His words, and those who stray from God's path bring death, scarcity, and hate. If you want to follow the one true shepherd, you just have to listen to Jesus's words.

11. HAVING INNER PEACE

"I have told you all this so that you may have peace in me. Here on earth, you will have many trials and sorrows. But take heart because I have overcome the world."

John 16:33

In the lives of human beings, there is conflict, sadness, and death. Many things separate us from happiness. Many false idols promise us things they cannot deliver. Only Jesus can give us peace and true happiness. When you follow God's path, true inner peace fills your heart with joy and contentment. Jesus defeated evil in the world with His resurrection and showed us the way to eternal salvation.

12. LOVING GOD

"You shall love the Lord your God with all your heart, and with all your soul, and with all your mind." This is the main and greatest commandment. The second is equally important: "Love your neighbor as yourself." All the law and all the demands of the prophets are based on these two commandments.

Matthew 22:36-40

The word of God, the teachings of Jesus, and the life of every Christian are based on one thing: love. First, the unconditional love for God, the Father, and creator of all things. Second: love for others, who are children of the same God and, therefore, your siblings. That love for the Father must be genuine, without any doubts whatsoever. It must be based on firm faith and sincere love. All other laws of holy men and women of all times are founded on these two principles.

13. FOCUS ON THE PRESENT MOMENT

"Do not worry about tomorrow, for tomorrow will bring its own worries. The worry of today is enough for today."

Matthew 6:34

Jesus tells us in this passage: worry about today, do not suffer about tomorrow. Many of us suffer for what is coming next, for illnesses or problems that we do not have. Others live distressed, thinking about a death that may take years to come. They do not enjoy or focus on the present because their minds are worried about a future that may never come. The Son of God invites us to concentrate on today and not suffer for tomorrow. If you wish to live the present with all its intensity and beauty, you should focus on what is, not on what could be.

14. TAKE UP YOUR CROSS

"If any of you want to be my follower, you must turn from your selfish ways, take up your cross, and follow me. For whoever wishes to save his life will lose it; but the one who loses his life for my sake will save it."

Mark 8:34-35

To be able to follow the way of Jesus, the path of life, love, and eternal salvation, you have to overcome your own selfishness. Put aside your worries, your sadness, and your joy, and focus on serving others. Then, when adopting the way of Jesus, you will find true life—the life of salvation.

15. WATER OF LIFE

"Everyone who drinks this water will be thirsty again, but whoever drinks the water I give him will never thirst; indeed, the water I give him will become in him a spring of water welling up to eternal life."

John 4:13-14

God, through the words of Jesus, frees us from the tyranny of time and opens the way for us to eternity. This is His promise, and it is also the hope, the signs of which we discover in advance in the loving and deep encounter with others, in the experience of the water of life and love.

16. GOD'S CARE FOR PEOPLE

"What do you think? If a man has a hundred sheep, and one of them goes astray, does he not leave the ninety-nine and go to the mountains to seek the one that is straying? And if he finds it, I truly tell you, he is happier with that sheep than he is with the ninety-nine that did not stray. In the same way, your Father who is in heaven is not willing that any of these little ones should perish."

Matthew 18:12-14

The love of God is directed towards all people. This means that He loves both each person and humanity in general, that is to say, He loves you and everyone else. The practice of this love leads Him to care not only for those who stay with Him but also for those who move away temporarily. Hence, instead of leaving those who stray to their fate, He finds a way to bring them back to His fold. For that reason, although at times you may feel that you are far away from God, do not forget that He will always seek you and wait with His arms wide open: reuniting with you is a reason for His greatest joy.

17. ATTENTION TO SINNERS

"Those who are well have no need of a physician, but those who are sick. I did not come to call the righteous, but sinners, to repentance."
                                        Luke 5:31-32

If it were about summoning only the righteous, God's task would be simple, but it would be limited to gathering those who, due to their holiness, have already answered the call of Jesus and are willing to follow Him. But God's love is universal, which means that it is addressed to every person. For that reason, His concern is focused on bringing back those who have drifted away from Him, because they are the ones who need immediate divine attention and redemption. Thus, when you are feeling bad for any behavior, do not forget that Jesus is always willing to forgive you if you repent.

18. DISPOSITION TO SERVE

"For the Son of Man did not come to be served, but to serve, and give his life as a ransom for many."

Mark 10:45

Contrary to what might be expected, Jesus does not appear before us with the usual attitude of those in power. Instead of turning people into objects under His dominion for His benefit, He, even being powerful, places Himself at the service of others. This disposition reaches a supreme dimension, as He offers His life for the redemption of all people. It is necessary for such an attitude of Jesus to be present in your life and for service to others to be a fundamental guide for the various activities that you undertake.

19. DO NOT BE ASHAMED OF JESUS

"What good is it to gain the world if you are going to lose your soul? Is there anything more valuable than your soul? Whoever is ashamed of me and of my words in these faithless and sinful days, the Son of Man will be ashamed of that person when he comes in his Father's glory with the holy angels."

Mark 8:36-38

The insatiable desire for power that drives those who control and, at the same time, are controlled by the powers of the world results in the loss of what is most valuable: the soul. Losing the soul means to distance oneself from God to the point of being ashamed of Him and, consequently, falling into the domain of sin. Build your attitude in your relationship with yourself and others, guided by the purity of Christian love, so you do not lose your soul and never be ashamed of Jesus.

20. VIOLENCE AND THE KINGDOM OF GOD

"My kingdom is not of this world. If my kingdom were of this world, my servants would fight, so that I would not be delivered to the Jews; but now My kingdom is not from here."

John 18:36

God's kingdom has a unique nature, with a logic distinct from that of earthly kingdoms. That is why the attitude of Jesus' followers differs from what might be expected in human beings. Instead of resorting to violence, they resist it, which represents a significant departure from what is typical in human conflicts. This countercurrent position, implicitly woven together with the principle of treating others as we want to be treated, is based on the Christian supremacy of love for one's neighbor. Ensure that your relationships with others are always guided by the spirit of non-violence that should characterize Christians.

21. DO NOT JUDGE

"Do not judge, and you will not be judged. For with the same judgment you pronounce, you will be judged, and with the measure you use, it will be measured to you. Why do you see the speck that is in your brother's eye, but do not notice the beam that is in your own eye? How can you say to your brother, 'Let me remove the speck from your eye,' when there is a beam in your own eye? You hypocrite, first take the beam out of your own eye, and then you will see clearly to remove the speck from your brother's eye."

Matthew 7:1-5

All people are sinners, and we can all make mistakes that distance us from God. For this reason, no one can claim the authority to judge others. Instead of focusing on others' faults, you should examine your own faults. All of this demonstrates God's mercy, who, being aware of our human weaknesses, is always open to forgiveness. Let this example become the foundation and guide for your relationships with others and with yourself.

22. GO TO GOD

"Ask, and it will be given to you; seek, and you will find; knock, and the door will be opened to you. Which of you, if your son asks for bread, will give him a stone? Or if he asks for a fish, will give him a snake? If you, then, being evil, know how to give good gifts to your children, how much more will your heavenly Father give good things to those who ask Him!"

Matthew 7:7-11

Like all children in relation to their parents, people are not alone or helpless in the world; they can always count on the help and support of God. It is enough to express our desire to be in contact with Him through prayer or other diverse ways to connect with the divine. In this openness, His great love for us is revealed. Thus, turn to God whenever you need Him. If we, as imperfect beings, attend to our children, how much more will God attend to us, being the perfect Father.

23. PROVIDENCE

"Do not worry about your life, what you will eat or what you will drink, or about your body, what you will wear. Is not life more valuable than food, and the body more valuable than clothing? Look at the birds of the air: they neither sow nor reap nor gather into barns, and yet your heavenly Father feeds them. Are you not more valuable than they?"

Matthew 6:25-31

Concerns about meeting the needs of daily life can often be overwhelming. We desire control over our lives, to shape and guide events according to our will and expectations. This attention is necessary, as the continuity of our existence depends on it. However, when it becomes excessive, we may forget that all aspects of reality, including the elements with which we sustain and clothe ourselves, come from God and have been given to us by Him. If our lives revolve around such matters, we can lose sight of what is essential: the poetry of existence, enveloped by the divine.

24. COMMUNICATING WITH GOD

"Again, truly I tell you that if two of you on earth agree about anything they ask for, it will be done for them by my Father in heaven. For where two or three gather in my name, there am I with them."

Matthew 18:19-20

Although the relationship with God begins personally, it is not the only way it can develop. Beyond the individual relationship is the experience that connects us with the divine presence, a dual experience: on one hand, that which unites us as members of the same faith and, on the other, that which connects us to God as a whole. Strive to combine the various ways of communicating with God so that your spiritual experience is filled with fullness.

25. PRINCIPLE OF FAITH

"Now Thomas, one of the Twelve, called the Twin, was not with them when Jesus came. So, the other disciples told him, 'We have seen the Lord.' But he said to them, 'Unless I see in his hands the mark of the nails and place my finger into the mark of the nails, and place my hand into his side, I will never believe.' Eight days later, his disciples were inside again, and Thomas was with them. Although the doors were locked, Jesus came and stood among them and said, 'Peace be with you.' Then he said to Thomas, 'Put your finger here, and see my hands; and put out your hand and place it in my side. Do not disbelieve but believe.' Thomas answered him, 'My Lord and my God!' Jesus said to him, 'Have you believed because you have seen me? Blessed are those who have not seen and yet have believed.'"

John 20:24-29

At times, doubt may plague our lives, leading us to demand evidence in search of a definitive explanation for our experiences as Christians. This neglects the meaning and essence of faith. Having faith means accepting the truth of Jesus without requiring any proof beyond that contained in His word. Thus, rather than seeing to believe, it is about believing to see – to joyfully discover the unfathomable spiritual dimension underpinned by His promise.

26. BREAD OF LIFE

"I am the bread of life. Your ancestors ate the manna in the wilderness, and they died; this is the bread that comes down from heaven, so that whoever eats this bread shall not die. I am the living bread that has come down from heaven, whoever eats this bread will live forever; and the bread that I will give is my flesh, which I will give for the life of the world."

John 6:48-51

Jesus sacrifices his life for the lives of humanity. This is the central aspect of the salvation process. However, this sacrifice attains its full meaning in the resurrection. Through this event, it becomes evident that death is not final, that it does not have the last word, and that Jesus, the bread of life, provides us the opportunity to live forever. Always keep Jesus' promise in mind, and your life will be filled with joy and hope.

27. CHILDREN AND THE KINGDOM OF HEAVEN

"Truly I tell you, unless you change and become like little children, you will never enter the kingdom of heaven. Therefore, whoever becomes as humble as this child is the greatest in the kingdom of heaven. And whoever welcomes one such child in my name welcomes me. If anyone causes one of these little ones who believe in me to stumble, it would be better for them to have a large millstone hung around their neck and to be drowned in the depths of the sea."

Matthew 18:3-6

The promise of salvation through Jesus necessitates profound transformation. One must become like a child, which entails rediscovering the deep spirituality characteristic of childhood. Children hold a privileged place in Jesus' teachings, as they embody the essential innocence required to enter the Kingdom of Heaven. Therefore, they are under God's special protection and must also be protected by humanity.

28. FOLLOWING JESUS

"As Jesus was walking beside the Sea of Galilee, he saw two brothers, Simon called Peter and his brother Andrew. They were casting a net into the lake, for they were fishermen. Jesus said, 'Come, follow me, and I will make you fishers of men.' At once they left their nets and followed him."

Matthew 4:18-20

God's will manifests in the world in mysterious ways. Simon and Andrew, who probably believed that their lives' destinies were already determined as fishermen, responded immediately to Jesus' call without any hesitation. His words were enough to transform them from fishermen to fishers of men, embarking on a journey that would take them from their peaceful existence in Galilee into the wider world. This demonstrates that nothing in life is definitive, and it is always possible for God to draw near and invite us to enter His service. For this reason, you must remain open and receptive.

29. THE NOVELTY OF JESUS

"No one pours new wine into old wineskins; otherwise, the wine will burst the skins, and both the wine and the skins will be ruined. Instead, new wine must be poured into new wineskins."

Mark 2:22

Jesus offered the world a new truth, partly because it represented something quite different from the Jewish tradition (the old wineskins), and also because it was open to embracing people from various cultures and traditions. This is part of the promise of salvation for all humanity. That is why, despite the time that has passed since Jesus' arrival, his word still carries a sense of novelty and resonates with his closeness to all of us, inviting us to his table.

Let's be open to receiving the ever-renewed word of Jesus.

30. RELIGIOUS FORMALISM

"The Sabbath was made for man, not man for the Sabbath; so, the Son of Man is lord even of the Sabbath."

Mark 2:27-28

Institutional forms have the purpose of facilitating the encounter between humans and God, providing necessary assistance and creating appropriate conditions. However, it must not be forgotten that "the Son of Man is lord even of the Sabbath," meaning that rules must be infused with the love with which Jesus approaches us. May your words and actions radiate joy and supreme understanding to those around you.

31. THE ENCOUNTER WITH FAITH

"With what can we compare the kingdom of God, or what parable shall we use for it? It is like a mustard seed, which, when sown upon the ground, is the smallest of all the seeds on earth; yet when it is sown, it grows up and becomes the greatest of all shrubs, and puts forth large branches, so that the birds of the air can make nests in its shade."

Mark 4:30-32

Although it is a transcendent event, the encounter with faith does not happen instantaneously. Not everyone becomes a believer in a single moment, and faith does not arrive like an object packaged in a box with precise instructions for use. The journey to faith is subtle and mysterious, involving a sower and a seed as humble as a mustard seed. It also requires our presence as receptive soil. Then, what was small and modest becomes a dazzling and beautiful plant.

May you be open to the encounter with faith, allowing you to one day become a plant whose branches provide shelter for the birds of the sky.

32. FORGIVE YOUR NEIGHBOR

"If your brother sins against you, rebuke him, and if he repents, forgive him. If he sins against you seven times in a day, and seven times comes back to you saying, 'I repent,' you must forgive him."

Luke 17:3-4

God is willing to forgive us for our repeated sins. It does not matter how many times we fall into them. Beyond sin, our relationship with God is marked by forgiveness because it encompasses the love that God has for us. In the same way, we should treat our neighbors: regardless of the number of times they may wrong us, we must forgive them. Having received God's forgiveness for our sins, we can hardly deny forgiveness to our neighbors.

33. HUMAN STRUGGLE AND PROVIDENCE

"Do not worry, saying, 'What shall we eat?' or 'What shall we drink?' or 'What shall we wear?' For the pagans run after all these things, and your heavenly Father knows that you need them. But seek first his kingdom and his righteousness, and all these things will be given to you as well. Therefore do not worry about tomorrow, for tomorrow will worry about itself."

Matthew 6:31-34

Jesus teaches that what is essential for Christians is to contribute to the creation of the Kingdom of God. Everything else, related to our material existence, has secondary importance. This does not mean that it is not essential for our existence: we need to eat, sleep, and have a place to live with dignity. However, God, knowing our needs, ensures that they are met, so we must not let them distract us from what is truly important: preparing for our final encounter with Him.

34. FAITH AND THE POWER OF JESUS

"A man with leprosy came and knelt before him and said, 'Lord, if you are willing, you can make me clean.' Jesus reached out his hand and touched the man. 'I am willing,' he said. 'Be clean!' Immediately he was cleansed of his leprosy."

Matthew 8:2-3

The numerous Gospel stories that depict Jesus' miraculous acts reflect the logic that governs the encounter with faith and divine mercy and power. Men and women approach Him with the hope that He will resolve situations that, by human common sense, seem impossible to solve. Jesus welcomes them, listens to their requests, and grants them what they ask for through the power of His word.

Let us never forget that Jesus is the embodiment of love and that He is always ready to help us in our time of need.

35. SIN, PUNISHMENT AND THE SECOND COMMANDMENT

"The scribes and the Pharisees brought a woman caught in adultery and placed her in their midst. They said to him, 'Teacher, this woman was caught in the act of adultery. In the Law, Moses commanded us to stone such women. So what do you say?' They said this to test him, so that they might have some charge to bring against him. Jesus bent down and wrote with his finger on the ground. When they persisted in questioning him, he straightened up and said to them, 'Let anyone among you who is without sin be the first to throw a stone at her.' And once again, he bent down and wrote on the ground. When they heard it, they went away, one by one, beginning with the oldest, until Jesus was left alone with the woman standing before him. Jesus straightened up and said to her, 'Woman, where are they? Has no one condemned you?' She said, 'No one, sir.' Jesus said, 'Neither do I condemn you. Go your way, and from now on do not sin again.'"

John 8:3-11

We are all sinners, and no one has the right to judge or inflict violence upon others because of their sins. Given God's immense love for humanity, punishment is replaced by Jesus' gentle words, which encourage us to leave sin behind and follow the path of holiness. This does not mean to violate the second commandment; instead, always remember the value of this principle: "Love your neighbor as yourself."

36. IGNORANCE AND SIN

"When they came to the place called The Skull, they crucified him there, along with the criminals—one on his right, the other on his left. Jesus said, 'Father, forgive them, for they do not know what they are doing.' And they divided up his clothes by casting lots."

Luke 23:33-34

Although sin originates from evil, ignorance enables it. We enable evil simply by not knowing what is good. Thus, Jesus, even in the midst of his immense and unjust suffering, asks his Father to forgive his tormentors instead of punishing them harshly.

Let us ask God for the ability to recognize evil so that we never become its instrument.

37. SHARING BREAD AND WINE

"When the hour came, Jesus and his apostles reclined at the table. And he said to them, 'I have eagerly desired to eat this Passover with you before I suffer. For I tell you, I will not eat it again until it finds fulfillment in the kingdom of God.' After taking the cup, he gave thanks and said, 'Take this and divide it among you. For I tell you I will not drink again from the fruit of the vine until the kingdom of God comes.' And he took bread, gave thanks and broke it, and gave it to them, saying, 'This is my body given for you; do this in remembrance of me.' In the same way, after the supper he took the cup, saying, 'This cup is the new covenant in my blood, which is poured out for you.'"

Luke 22:14-20

Jesus knows that his death is near and wants to meet with his disciples for what will be their last supper together. At first, this act seems to be an ending: he will not eat or drink again, and some of his gestures are meant to be remembered. However, this end is only apparent or rather a moment of transition between the present world and the Kingdom of God, between what is marked by expiration and suffering, and the definitive and true life that Jesus promises us with his New Covenant.

Let us always remember that the power of love conquers death, and let us rejoice in knowing that the day will come when we will all gather together and share our wine and bread with God and with all people.

38. GOD'S WILL AND HIS WORK

"Meanwhile, his disciples urged him, 'Rabbi, eat something.' But he said to them, 'I have food to eat that you know nothing about.' Then his disciples said to each other, 'Could someone have brought him food?' Jesus said, 'My food is to do the will of him who sent me and to finish his work.'"

John 4:31-34

As in other passages, Jesus uses an analogy to reveal his mission. His daily bread is not the usual food focused on maintaining and developing bodily processes, but something more profound spiritually speaking: to do the will of God the Father and finish his work. This indication points to the definition of the Christian sense of work, characterized by reciprocity. Whoever works for the construction of the Kingdom of God does not have to sacrifice themselves and is not subject to any destructive fatigue; instead, they find their full realization in work. Thus, just like Jesus, they feed on what they do in order to fulfill God's will. Participate in the construction of the Divine Kingdom, and you will experience what will fill you with eternal reality.

39. SHELTER FROM GREED

"'Take heed and beware of any kind of greed: for a man's life consists not in the abundance of the things which he possesses.' And he told them this parable: 'The ground of a certain rich man yielded an abundant harvest. He thought to himself, "What shall I do? I have no place to store my crops." Then he said, "This is what I will do. I will tear down my barns and build bigger ones, and there I will store my surplus grain. And I will say to myself, 'You have plenty of grain laid up for many years. Take life easy; eat, drink, and be merry.'" But God said to him, "You fool! This very night your life will be demanded from you. Then who will get what you have prepared for yourself? This is how it will be with whoever stores up things for themselves but is not rich toward God."'"

Luke 12:15-21

It is necessary to give a fair value to riches, as they can generate a kind of madness and make us lose our proper perspective on life. What is the point of accumulating when it becomes an end in itself? The character in the parable thinks that he has already reached a point where he can be free from work and, detaching from all worries, he wants to simply enjoy life. However, riches are fragile and are condemned to destruction. That is why Jesus proposes to grow rich in the dimension of what is immutable and true, that is, by living a Christian life.

40. PERSECUTIONS AND ETERNAL LIFE

"Blessed are those persecuted for righteousness' sake, for theirs is the Kingdom of God. Blessed are you when they insult you, persecute you, and utter every kind of evil against you falsely because of me. Rejoice and be glad, for your reward is great in heaven, for so men persecuted the prophets who were before you."

Matthew 5:10-12

Embracing the Christian condition means upholding and defending the truth and justice, which often involves various risks. From Jesus' crucifixion at Calvary to the present day, many have been persecuted, insulted, slandered, and more, simply for being his followers. However, we must never forget that Jesus is always with us to face these circumstances. For this reason, there is no need to be afraid. Jesus' love overcomes hate and offers us his promise of eternal bliss.

41. CHARITY

"When you give alms, do not let your left hand know what your right hand is doing, so that your alms may be in secret; and your Father who sees in secret will reward you."

Matthew 6:3

The true sense of solidarity that Christianity promotes must lead us to lend our support and help to those who need it, often as vulnerable as Christ at Calvary. However, this action should not become an opportunity for boasting and ostentation. It is not human beings who have to judge our actions, but God the Father, the perfect judge who expects the best from us.

42. RELIEF OF JESUS

"Come to me, all you who are weary and burdened, and I will give you rest."

Matthew 11:28

On certain occasions, life's challenges seem to weigh us down, problems arise simultaneously, and we feel overwhelmed. In those moments, we should not forget that Jesus invites us to turn to him for support and relief whenever we need it. Therefore, when sadness, loneliness, and desperation gather in your soul, never forget that Jesus loves you and he is waiting for you to help.

43. SPIRIT OF PEACE

"You have heard that it was said, 'An eye for an eye, and a tooth for a tooth.' But I tell you, do not resist an evil person. If anyone slaps you on your right cheek, turn to them the other cheek also. And if anyone wants to sue you and take your shirt, hand over your coat as well. If anyone forces you to go one mile, go with them two miles."

Matthew 5:38-41

Do not resist evil, do not oppose violence with the same arguments of violence, thereby perpetuating the cycle of aggression and suffering. This is one of the most significant features that distinguish the Christian spirit from the older Jewish law. Instead of using violence, we must respond with love. This way, if in certain circumstances we do not know how to face those who harm us, remember that as Christians, we are committed to following the way of Jesus, which is the path of peace among people.

44. THE KINGDOM OF HEAVEN IS WITHIN YOU

"Once, on being asked by the Pharisees when the Kingdom of God would come, Jesus replied, 'The coming of the Kingdom of God is not something that can be observed, nor will people say, "Here it is," or "There it is," because the Kingdom of God is in your midst.'"

Luke 17:20-21

The Kingdom of God is not like the kingdoms of men, and strictly speaking, it is not limited to a specific place or moment within time and space. Its spiritual nature does not correspond to these coordinates; rather, it refers to a dimension involving those who live the Christian experience to the fullest depth. For this reason, the experience of the Kingdom of God can be brought forward, depending on how we live our Christianity in relation to others. In this sense, living in the presence of the Kingdom of God within us now means tasting in advance what God has prepared for us in eternal life.

45. FRATERNAL JOY OF LIFE

"Surely the bridegroom's attendants cannot fast while the bridegroom is still with them? As long as they have the bridegroom with them, they cannot fast. But the days will come when the bridegroom will be taken away from them, and on that day, they will fast."

John 2:19-20

It is necessary to give proper value to life. Even though it is transitory and simply leads us to the definitive and true existence, encountering others should be a reason for rejoicing because of the presence of Jesus among us. Thank God for allowing you to share your journey in the world with those around you, and always be a source of wholesome joy that attests to the presence of the spirit each time we meet with others.

44. FULFILLMENT OF GOD'S WILL

"Here are my mother and my brothers! For whoever does the will of my Father in heaven is my brother and sister and mother."

Mark 3:34-35

Jesus emphasizes the importance of family ties, as evidenced by the various references to the subject in many passages of the Gospel. However, he proposes that above all the relationships confined to a specific social bond, there is a system that unites believers. The foundation of this system is none other than the fulfillment of God's will, which establishes a fraternity based on the actions of faith. Always keep in mind, in any circumstance, the dimension that makes us all children of God globally, and ensure that your actions always align with the realization of the divine will.

45. TRUST IN GOD

"Why are you so afraid? Do you still have no faith?"

Mark 4:40

While Jesus was sleeping, a storm arose and was about to capsize the boat in which he was traveling. Those with him woke him up and asked him to stop the boat from sinking. Then Jesus stood up, commanded the sea to be still, and calmness ensued. He then spoke the words mentioned above. Fear, in a way, is an enemy of human beings because it can paralyze us and prevent us from acting. Fear is also an affront to God. Instead of entrusting ourselves to His protection, we seem to doubt His omnipotence. Therefore, instead of being consumed by fear, trust confidently in God's power and His love for us. He is your best support.

46. TRUTH WILL SET YOU FREE

"If you hold to my teaching, you are really my disciples. Then you will know the truth, and the truth will set you free."

John 8:31-32

As the scene at Calvary reveals, the root of evil is planted in ignorance. Human beings sin because they are not fully aware of the consequences of their actions. This condition changes when one becomes a disciple of Jesus, as this allows them to be in touch with His truth and gain a deeper understanding of sin. Thus, the liberating nature of Jesus' word: through it, the human being has the opportunity to emerge from the darkness that surrounds them and draw closer to God. Keep yourself open to the spiritual light that God provides, so you may experience the beauty of true freedom.

NEVER FORGET THIS

When everyone abandons you, Jesus will be with you.
When you don't know what to do, follow the way of Jesus.
When you feel sad, alone, and desperate, remember that Jesus loves you.
When in doubt, follow the word of Jesus.
When you are offended, remain calm and respond with love and understanding.
Help those who suffer, give bread to the hungry and water to the thirsty.
When someone you love dies, remember that death is only a transition, a door to reunite with the souls of those we love.
May your actions speak louder than your words,
and everything you do contribute to building a better world.
If Jesus walks beside you, you have no reason to fear.
Love always conquers hate, and joy overcomes sadness.